Tom's Big Pie

By Cameron Macintosh

In six days, it will be Pie Day at Tom's school.

The kids will bring pies.

"No one's pie will be as big as my pie!" said Tom.

At home, Tom said,
"Mum! Dad!
I must bring a big, big pie
for Pie Day!"

"What kind of pie, Tom?"
said Mum.

"What kind of pie filling
have we got?" said Tom.

"Here's some crust," said Dad.

"Let's put these wild plums in a pie," said Mum.

"No, thanks, Mum," said Tom.

Tom went off to think.

"I must bring a big pie,"
he said.
"But what can I find
to go in it?"

Tom had a sly plan.

He put some socks
in the pie dish.

Then he got one of Dad's ties!

He sat the crust on top.

Pie Crust

"That is a **big** pie!" said Tom.

On Pie Day, the kids loved Tom's big pie.

"That's such a big pie!" yelled Nat.

"Yum!" said Sky.
"I want to try some!"

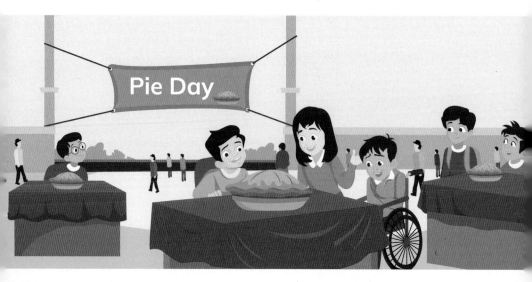

Sky cut into Tom's pie.

"Tom, why did you make
a sock pie?" Sky said.
"This pie is a big **lie**!"

"My pie **is** a lie," said Tom,
with a grin.
"But it is very big!"

CHECKING FOR MEANING

1. What did Mum say could go in Tom's pie? *(Literal)*

2. What did Tom put in his pie? *(Literal)*

3. Why was Tom's plan *sly*? *(Inferential)*

EXTENDING VOCABULARY

crust	What is the *crust* of a pie? What other foods have a crust? How can you describe a crust? Is it crunchy, soft, chewy, crispy?
wild	What are *wild* plums? How do they grow?
sly	What does *sly* mean? If you do something that is sly, is it clever?

MOVING BEYOND THE TEXT

1. If you were making a pie, what would you put in the filling?

2. Make a list of the fillings that usually go in a pie. What is your favourite? Why?

3. Have you ever done anything that is sly? What was it?

4. Foxes are often described as sly. What do they do?

SPELLINGS FOR THE LONG /i/ VOWEL SOUND

i	igh	i_e	y	ie

PRACTICE WORDS

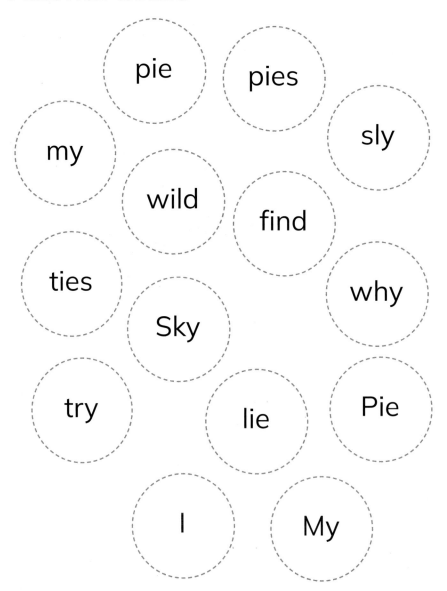

pie

pies

sly

my

wild

find

ties

why

Sky

try

lie

Pie

I

My